MACHINES CLOSE-UP

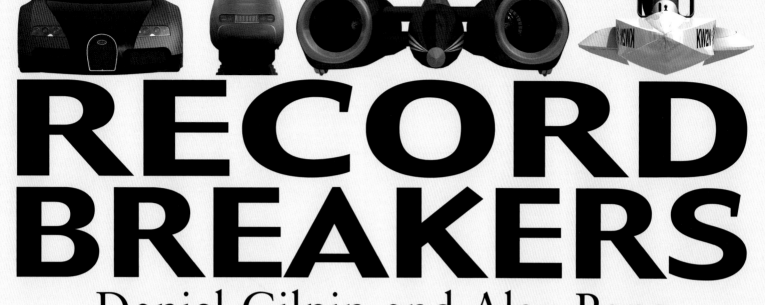

RECORD BREAKERS

Daniel Gilpin and Alex Pang

Marshall Cavendish
Benchmark

New York

This edition first published in 2011 in the United States by
Marshall Cavendish Benchmark

An imprint of Marshall Cavendish Corporation

Website: www.marshallcavendish.us

This publication represents the opinions and views of the author based
on Daniel Gilpin's and Alex Pang's personal experience, knowledge, and
research.
The information in this book serves as a general guide only. The author
and publisher have used their best efforts in preparing this book and
disclaim liability rising directly and indirectly from the use and application
of this book.

Other Marshall Cavendish Offices:
Marshall Cavendish International (Asia) Private Limited, 1 New Industrial
Road, Singapore 536196 • Marshall Cavendish International (Thailand) Co
Ltd. 253 Asoke, 12th Flr, Sukhumvit 21 Road, Klongtoey Nua, Wattana,
Bangkok 10110, Thailand • Marshall Cavendish (Malaysia) Sdn Bhd, Times
Subang, Lot 46, Subang Hi-Tech Industrial Park, Batu Tiga, 40000 Shah
Alam, Selangor Darul Ehsan, Malaysia

Marshall Cavendish is a trademark of Times Publishing Limited

Copyright © 2009 David West Children's Books

Library of Congress Cataloging-in-Publication Data

Gilpin, Daniel.
Record breakers / Daniel Gilpin and Alex Pang.
p. cm.
Includes index.
Summary: "Reveals and discusses the intricate internal workings of record
breaking machines"--Provided by publisher.
ISBN 978-1-60870-113-1
1. Motor vehicles--Speed--Juvenile literature. 2. Aeronautics--Records--
Juvenile literature. 3. World records--Juvenile literature. I. Pang, Alex. II.
Title.
TL147.G547 2011
629.04'6--dc22
2009043260

First published in 2009 by Wayland
Hachette Children's Books
338 Euston Road
London NW1 3BH
Wayland Australia
Level 17/207 Kent Street
Sydney, NSW 2000

Produced by
David West ⚇ Children's Books
7 Princeton Court
55 Felsham Road
London SW15 1AZ

Editor: Katharine Pethick
Designer: Rob Shone
Illustrator: Alex Pang
Consultant: Steve Parker

The photographs in this book are used by permission and through the
courtesy of:
Abbreviations: t-top, m-middle, b-bottom, r-right,
l-left, c-center.
4-5, Castrol; 6tr, Andreas Praefcke; 6bl, Castrol, 6br,
Alfred John West; 7ml, 7bl, 7br, Castrol; 8t, U.S. Air Force;
8ml, NASA; 8mr, Przemyslaw Jahr; 8b, Joe Mabel; 9t,
NASA; 9m, DAMASA; 9bl, Jorfer; 9br, Castrol; 30t,
Arpingstone; 30ml, NASA; 30mr, Andreas Manuel
Rodriguez; 30b, Martin Roll

Printed in China
135642

CONTENTS

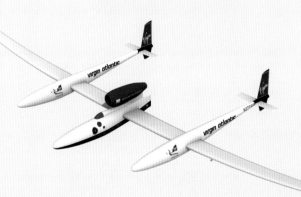

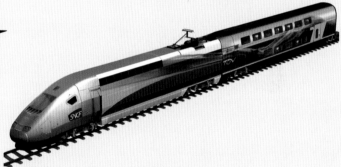
Glossary Words: when a word is printed in **bold**, you can look up its meaning in the Glossary on page 31.

INTRODUCTION

Some people like to take their machines to the limit—drive them hard to see exactly what they can do. But other, more adventuresome people see no limits and want to push the boundaries further. These are the people who design and build record breaking machines.

HOW TO USE THIS BOOK

MAIN TEXT

Gives details of the vehicle's history and explains which record it currently holds. Other information, such as when the record was set, is also covered here.

SPECIFICATIONS

Gives information about the vehicle's speed and dimensions.

CLOSE-UP VIEW

Details fascinating elements, vehicles, or equipment associated with the record breaker when it is in use.

TGV 4402

TGV 4402 is the fastest train ever to run on conventional rails. On April 3, 2007, it set a new world record speed of 357 mph (574.8 km/h). TGV 4402 is a one-of-a-kind train that was specially modified to make the world record attempt. It is based on the TGV POS, which routinely carries passengers through France at up to 198.8 mph (320 km/h).

TGV 4402
Length: 347 feet (106 meters)
Weight: 295 tons (268 metric tons)
Wheel diameter: 3.58 feet (1.092 meters)
Top speed: 357.1 mph (574.8 km/h)

BRAKES
TGV 4402 has disk brakes on its wheels and dynamic brakes on its axles. Together, these provide enough braking power to stop the train.

PANTOGRAPH
This is used to collect electric current from overhead lines in order to drive the train. Pantographs are commonly used by trains in France.

TRACK
Unlike the train, the tracks where the speed record was achieved was not modified in any way. It is a standard high speed train line.

DRIVER'S CAB
The cab of TGV 4402 has a comfortable, soft seat for the driver, surrounded by controls.

Cooling tanks

Pneumatic block

Upper deck

Lower deck

TRANSFORMERS
These convert the electrical power gathered by the pantograph to a voltage the train's engines can use.

28

POWER PACK
This receives electricity from the transformers and uses it to drive the wheels of the locomotive.

MOTOR BOGIE
Each of TGV 4402's two locomotives sits on two of these. For the record attempt, two were added to one of the carriages. Despite their name, TGV motor bogies do not have their own motors—instead, they use a system of gears to transfer power from the power pack to the wheels.

DUPLEX CARRIAGES
Three of these double-decker carriages were used between two TGV locomotives to construct the record-breaking train.

Permanent magnet motor

Secondary suspension

Primary suspension

29

MAIN ILLUSTRATION

Shows the internal structure of the vehicle and gives information on the positions of its various working parts.

INTERESTING FEATURES

Contains a detailed illustration of the engine or other design features that make the vehicle unique. Informative text explains the feature's function.

PAST RECORDS

WRIGHT FLYER III
In 1905, this early plane took the air speed record after flying at 34.8 mph (56 km/h).

Records come and records go. Most of the record-breaking vehicles of today are just the latest in a long line of title holders.

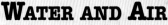

FIRST MOTOR VEHICLES

Theoretically, the land speed record for wheeled vehicles can be traced back to the chariots of Rome. However, most authorities begin their lists with motor vehicles. The earliest motor vehicle, the Benz Motorwagen, was built in 1885. Today's record holder is almost one hundred times faster.

BENZ MOTORWAGEN
This was the first true motor car, which held the first motor car speed record—a staggeringly slow 8 mph (13 km/h).

WATER AND AIR

Before the invention of the steam engine, water speed records were held and broken by sailing vessels. Air speed records began with the first powered flight, around the start of the twentieth century. For years, airplanes remained slower than boats.

TURBINIA
In 1897, this steamship reached 39 mph (62.9 km/h), breaking the water speed record.

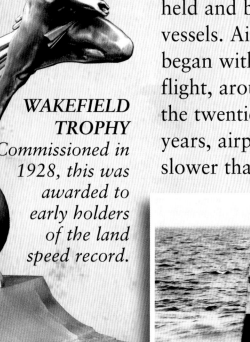

WAKEFIELD TROPHY
Commissioned in 1928, this was awarded to early holders of the land speed record.

BUILT FOR SPEED

When the first motor vehicles were built, speed was not really a consideration. It was more than a decade before cars were really tested to see how fast they could go. However, once cars got up to speed, the bug caught on. Even so, it would be the 1920s before cars could move faster than trains.

ELECTRICITY AND STEAM
In 1899, the electric La Jamais Contente (top) became the first vehicle to reach 62 mph (100 km/h). The steam-driven Stanley Rocket Racer (below) passed the 124 mph (200 km/h) mark in 1906.

GIANT SHIPS

Not all records are about speed—size is important too. This was demonstrated by the excitement surrounding the launch of the *Titanic*. In 1911, the ship's statistics were listed in newspapers all over the world.

RMS TITANIC
Weighing 58,583 tons (53,146 metric tons), this ship was the world's largest before it sank in 1912.

MISS ENGLAND II
In 1930, this British boat took the water speed record to 98.76 mph (158.94 km/h).

SUPERMARINE SEAPLANES
These were the fastest vehicles on Earth in 1931, with one reaching 407.49 mph (655.8 km/h).

SUNBEAM
In 1927, this car became the first to exceed 200 mph (322 km/h), when it was driven by Henry Segrave.

THE MODERN AGE

During the twentieth century, motor vehicles and aircraft increasingly became part of our lives. As their numbers grew, their design evolved and these vehicles became more efficient than before.

ME 262
This German jet took the air speed record in 1944, reaching 623.85 mph (1,004 km/h).

THE JET AGE

War provided the stimulus for ever faster aircraft. During World War II, German engineers developed the first jet engines. These took planes to speeds never dreamed of before.

BELL X-1
In 1947, this became the first manned vehicle to travel faster than the speed of sound.

BLUEBIRD CN7
In 1964, this Bluebird took the record for a four-wheeled car to 403.1 mph (648.73 km/h).

STREAMLINING

By the late 1920s, teams from both sides of the Atlantic were battling for the land speed record. Along with power, streamlining became an important feature. The competition between the United States and Europe also spread onto the water, with speed titles swapping hands every few years.

SLO-MO-SHUN IV
Piloted by Stan Sayres, this propeller-driven boat took the water speed record up to 178.45 mph (287.2 km/h) in 1952.

MILITARY MUSCLE

While the fastest cars and boats are built by civilians, the fastest aircraft have long been built for military use. Part of the reason for this is the massive cost involved in developing new aircraft. The SR-71 Blackbird program, for example, cost more than $1 billion.

ENDURANCE TESTS

Many modern records celebrate fuel economy and endurance rather than speed. One example of this is the battle to be fastest to fly around the globe without refueling.

SR-71 BLACKBIRD
This U.S. military aircraft holds the speed record for manned aircraft at 2,193 mph (3,530 km/h).

SHINKANSEN BULLET TRAINS
These Japanese trains set world record rail speeds in the 1960s and 1970s, and are still in use.

VOYAGER
In 1986, this aircraft, piloted by the American Dick Rutan, became the first to fly around the world without refueling.

THRUST 2
This car held the world land speed record from 1983 to 1997. Its driver, Richard Noble, developed the current record holder, the Thrust SSC.

LNER CLASS A4 MALLARD

Mallard was the fastest steam locomotive ever built. It set its record speed of 126 mph (203 km/h) in 1938. At that time Mallard was just five months old. Having remained in service with the London and North Eastern Railway (LNER) until 1963, it was restored to working order in the 1980s. It is now in the National Railway Museum in York, England.

STREAMLINED BODYWORK

Mallard's smooth shape helped increase its speed. It also enabled smoke from the chimney to be blown away from the driver's cab.

SMOKESTACK

Mallard had a Kylchap exhaust, which means excess steam and smoke from the firebox were mixed to create an even airflow through the fire tubes.

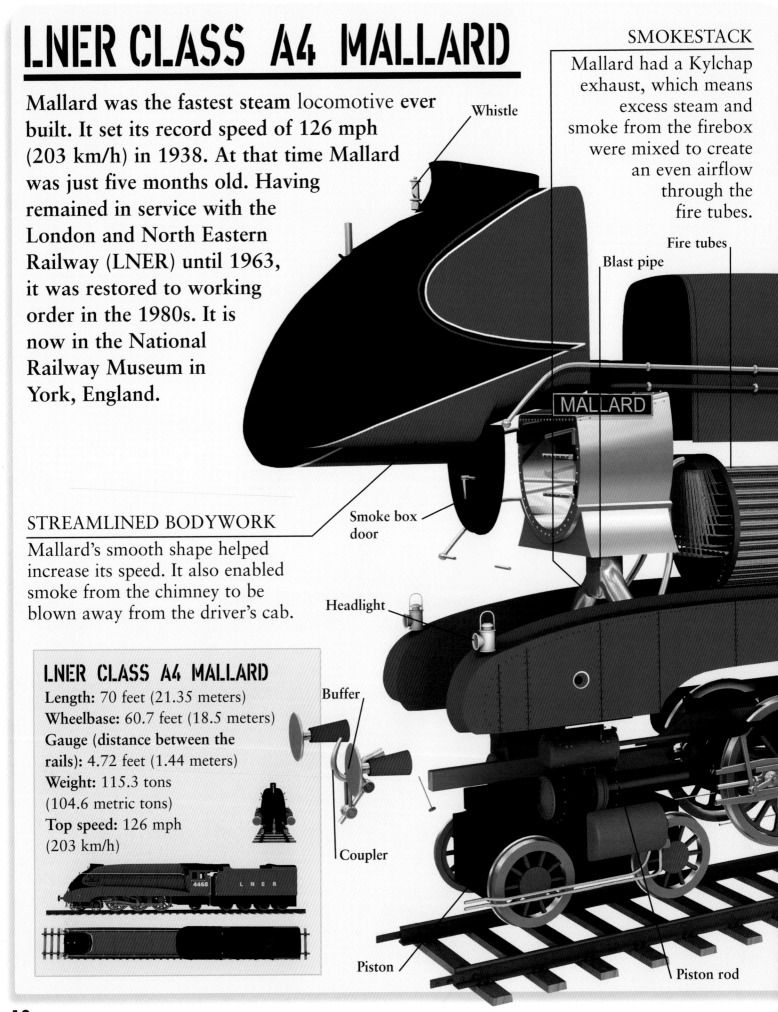

Whistle

Fire tubes

Blast pipe

MALLARD

Smoke box door

Headlight

Buffer

Coupler

Piston

Piston rod

LNER CLASS A4 MALLARD
Length: 70 feet (21.35 meters)
Wheelbase: 60.7 feet (18.5 meters)
Gauge (distance between the rails): 4.72 feet (1.44 meters)
Weight: 115.3 tons (104.6 metric tons)
Top speed: 126 mph (203 km/h)

BOILER

This held the water that was heated to make steam. Steam from the cylinders and smoke from the fire tubes collected in the smoke box in front, before going up through the chimney.

CYLINDERS

Mallard had three cylinders —two on the outside at the front of the locomotive and one on the inside between the two outside cylinders. The cylinders contained pistons, which were pushed out by the steam, and this in turn drove the wheels.

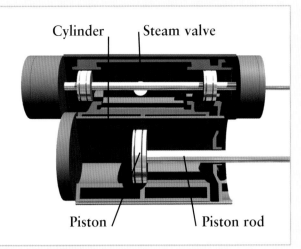

Cylinder   Steam valve

Piston   Piston rod

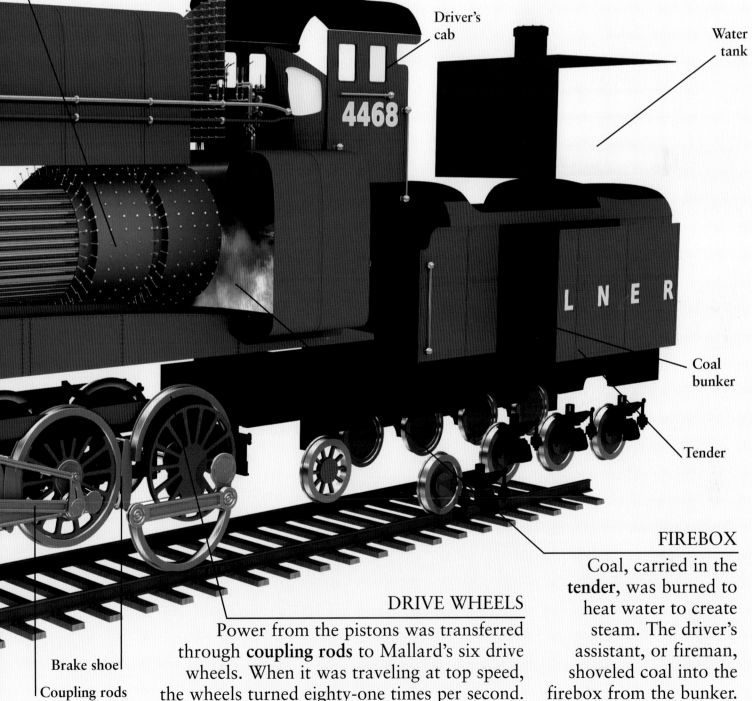

Driver's cab

4468

Water tank

L N E R

Coal bunker

Tender

Brake shoe

Coupling rods

DRIVE WHEELS

Power from the pistons was transferred through **coupling rods** to Mallard's six drive wheels. When it was traveling at top speed, the wheels turned eighty-one times per second.

FIREBOX

Coal, carried in the **tender**, was burned to heat water to create steam. The driver's assistant, or fireman, shoveled coal into the firebox from the bunker.

CRAWLER-TRANSPORTER

Built in 1965, NASA's Crawler-Transporters, named Franz and Hans, are the world's biggest self-powered vehicles. Their original job, at the Kennedy Space Center, was to carry the gigantic Saturn V rockets from the assembly buildings to the launch pad. In 1969, the Apollo 11 mission that took the first astronauts to the Moon began its long journey on the top of a Crawler.

DIESEL ENGINE GENERATORS

The main power for the Crawler comes from four **diesel** engines. These run generators that provide electricity for the motors, **hydraulic** pumps, lights, and ventilation fans.

HYDRAULIC PUMPS

The Crawler has twelve pumps. These force hydraulic fluid into the pistons that steer it and drive the jacking, equalizing, and leveling system that keeps the platform level.

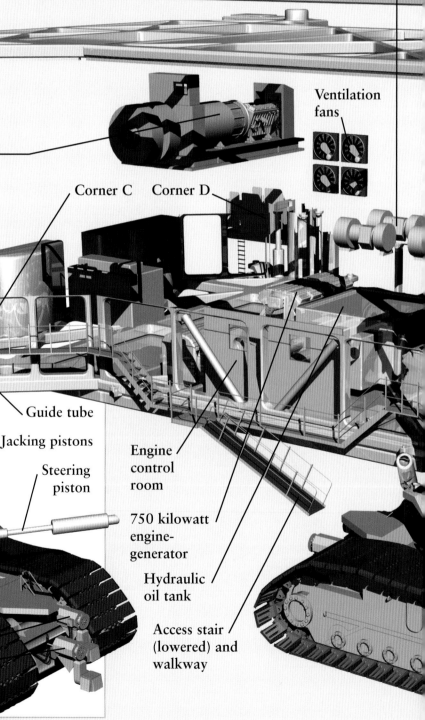

Ventilation fans

Corner C   Corner D

Engine control room

750 kilowatt engine-generator

Hydraulic oil tank

Access stair (lowered) and walkway

PROPULSION TRUCK

*Two Caterpillar tracks are driven by four **electric traction motors**. These move the Crawler along the 3.47 mile (5.6 kilometer) path or "crawlerway" from the assembly building to the launch pad—a journey that takes about five hours.*

Guide tube

Jacking pistons

Steering piston

Caterpillar shoes

Drive sprocket

Traction motors

FUEL TANK

The Crawler has two fuel tanks, each holding 5,019 gallons (19,000 liters) of diesel fuel. It uses 0.9 gallons (3.5 liters) of fuel to travel 42 feet (13 meters).

CRAWLER-TRANSPORTER

Length: 131 feet (40 meters)
Width: 115 feet (35 meters)
Height: 19-26 feet (6-8 meters)
Top speed: 2 mph (3.2 km/h) unloaded, 1 mph (1.6 km/h) loaded
Weight: 2,720 tons (2,468 metric tons)

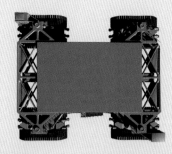

Platform

150 kilowatt engine-generator

Second 2,000 kilowatt engine-generator

Chassis top

Corner A

Corner B

WATER RADIATORS

The Crawler needs six radiators to stop its four diesel engines from overheating. Each radiator pumps out 502 gallons (1,900 liters) of water.

SPACE SHUTTLE

Since 1981, the Crawlers have been used to carry the Space Shuttle to the launch pad at the Kennedy Space Center. A laser is used to accurately position the Crawler beneath the Mobile Launcher Platform with the Shuttle on top. Hydraulic jacks then raise the Crawler and lift the platform and shuttle—a total weight of 5,511 tons (5,000 metric tons).

External liquid fuel tank

Solid rocket boosters

Space Shuttle

Crawler-Transporter

Mobile launcher platform

OPERATOR'S CAB

The Crawler has two operator's cabs—one on the front and one on the back. To reverse, the driver switches from the cab on corner B to corner D and drives away.

BEDE BD-5J

The Bede BD-5J is the world's smallest jet airplane. It was developed in 1973 from the Bede BD-5—a kit airplane that was powered by a rear propeller. The Bede BD-5J is no longer being made. However, a few are still able to fly so the U.S. Department of Defense has certified the design as a replacement aircraft for cruise missiles.

Canopy

COCKPIT
This has room for a single pilot. The large canopy gives great visibility and the seating position is comfortable.

AVIONICS
Like the rest of the plane, the **avionics** are miniaturized. The electronics extend to the fuel control system, which is fully automatic.

Instrument panel

BEDE BD-5J
Wingspan: 17 feet (5.2 meters)
Length: 12.4 feet (3.8 meters)
Height: 5.2 feet (1.6 meters)
Top speed: 299.5 mph (482 km/h)

UNDERCARRIAGE
The retractable landing gear, or **undercarriage**, is built into the fuselage. Although the two back wheels are close together, the system is stable.

Air intake

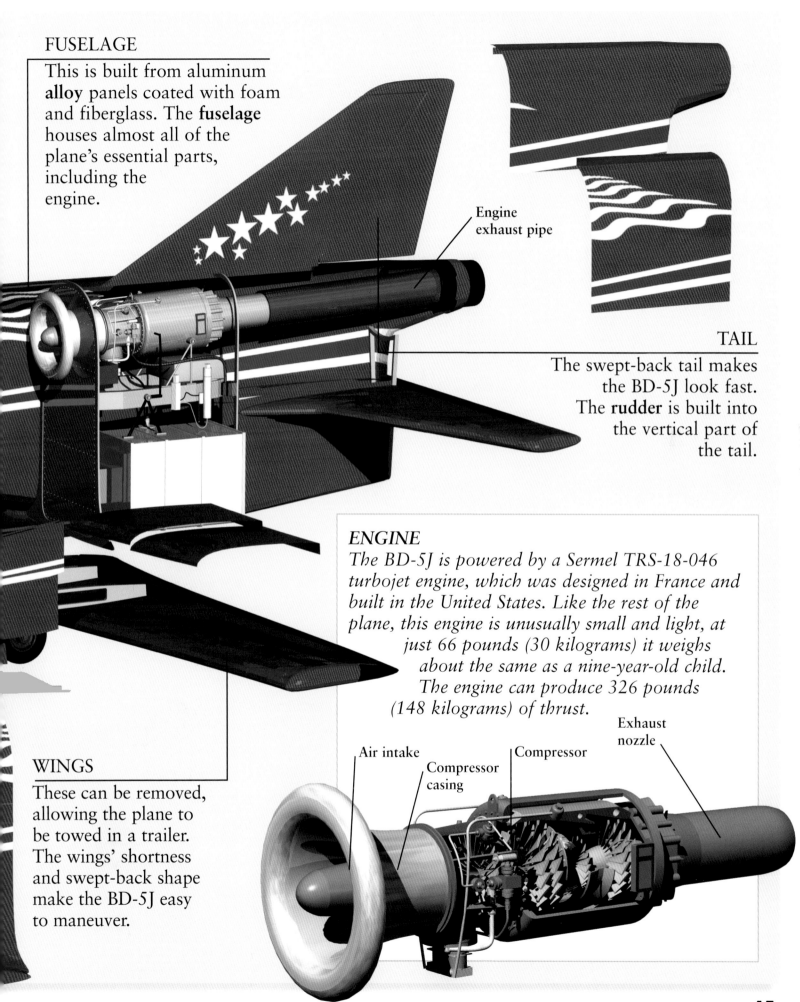

FUSELAGE

This is built from aluminum **alloy** panels coated with foam and fiberglass. The **fuselage** houses almost all of the plane's essential parts, including the engine.

Engine
exhaust pipe

TAIL

The swept-back tail makes the BD-5J look fast. The **rudder** is built into the vertical part of the tail.

ENGINE

The BD-5J is powered by a Sermel TRS-18-046 turbojet engine, which was designed in France and built in the United States. Like the rest of the plane, this engine is unusually small and light, at just 66 pounds (30 kilograms) it weighs about the same as a nine-year-old child. The engine can produce 326 pounds (148 kilograms) of thrust.

WINGS

These can be removed, allowing the plane to be towed in a trailer. The wings' shortness and swept-back shape make the BD-5J easy to maneuver.

Air intake

Compressor
casing

Compressor

Exhaust
nozzle

SPIRIT OF AUSTRALIA

Spirit of Australia is the current holder of the water speed record. The jet-powered boat set the record at 317.5 mph (511.1 km/h) in 1978, on the Blowering Dam reservoir in New South Wales, Australia. *Spirit of Australia* was piloted by Ken Warby. It is now kept at the Australian National Maritime Museum in Sydney.

SPIRIT OF AUSTRALIA

Length: 26.9 feet (8.2 meters)
Top speed: 317.5 mph (511.1 km/h)
Main structural material: wood

COCKPIT

This is fully enclosed by a glass canopy, which was added after the boat had already tested at 244.8 mph (394 km/h).

Fuel tank

Hull

KW2N

Air intakes

SPONSONS

These extra, miniature hulls are attached to the front of the boat. They give it greater stability when accelerating and help to lift the front off the water.

Low speed

High speed

HYDROPLANES

Spirit of Australia *is a hydroplane—a boat designed to travel with almost no contact with the water. Friction from contact with water slows a boat down. At full peed, only the rear tip of the hull touches the water's surface.*

16

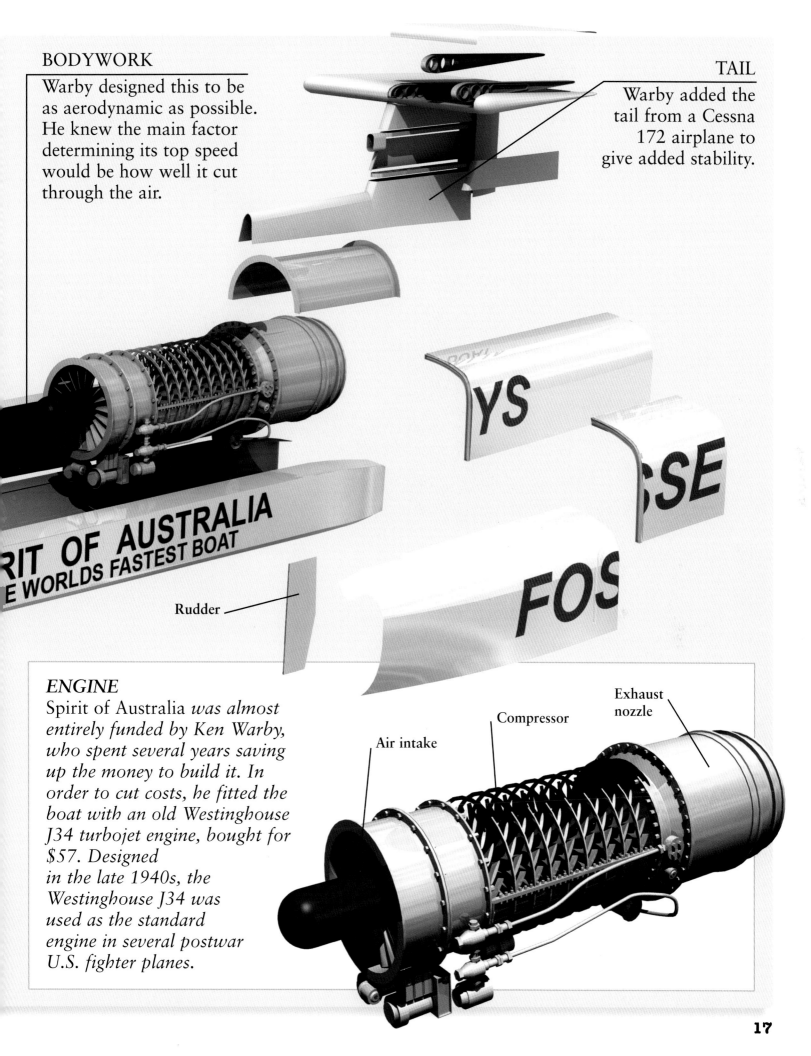

BODYWORK

Warby designed this to be as aerodynamic as possible. He knew the main factor determining its top speed would be how well it cut through the air.

TAIL

Warby added the tail from a Cessna 172 airplane to give added stability.

RIT OF AUSTRALIA
E WORLDS FASTEST BOAT

YS

SE

FOS

Rudder

ENGINE

Spirit of Australia *was almost entirely funded by Ken Warby, who spent several years saving up the money to build it. In order to cut costs, he fitted the boat with an old Westinghouse J34 turbojet engine, bought for $57. Designed in the late 1940s, the Westinghouse J34 was used as the standard engine in several postwar U.S. fighter planes.*

Air intake

Compressor

Exhaust nozzle

THRUST SSC

Thrust SSC is the current holder of the land speed record. SSC stands for supersonic **car**. Thrust SSC was the first land vehicle to **break** the sound barrier. When it set the record on October 15, 1997, it reached a staggering 763 mph (1,228 km/h). It was exactly fifty years and a day since Chuck Yeager became the first person to break the sound barrier in his Bell X-1 jet airplane.

FIRE CONTROL

In such a ground-breaking car, the risk of fire is always present. The Thrust SSC has heat sensors in the body of the vehicle and **infrared** sensors in its cockpit. Extinguishers are fitted around the body of the car.

Fuel tank

Air intake

Nose cone

COCKPIT

This is near the car's center of gravity and is entered through the removable canopy. Inside, the instrumentation includes an air speed indicator, converted from a Phantom jet plane's **gauge**.

THRUST SSC

Length: 54.1 feet (16.5 meters)
Height: 6.8 feet (2.1 meters)
Width: 12.1 feet (3.7 meters)
Weight: 11.5 tons (10.5 metric tons)
Top speed: 763 mph (1,228 km/h)

Tail

CHASSIS

The **chassis** is made from welded steel. The body panels are titanium, aluminum, and **carbon fiber**. Although the car is heavy, its weight is not a problem. The engines have the same power as about eight hundred Ford Focuses.

Parachute

AERODYNAMICS

Like a jet fighter, Thrust SSC has smooth lines to cut through the air. The tail gives downward force to keep it on the ground.

Engine housing

Canopy

ENGINE

Thrust SSC is powered by two Rolls-Royce Spey jet engines. The engines used during the record-breaking run at Black Rock Desert in Nevada were modified slightly by Rolls-Royce engineers to be even more powerful than standard Spey engines.

Air intake

Compressor

WHEELS

The car has solid aluminum alloy wheels. When the record was set, each one was rotating at more than 125 times per second.

Exhaust nozzle

X-43A

The X-43A is the world's fastest jet-powered aircraft. In November 2004, it set a new record speed of Mach 9.6, or around 6,999 mph (11,265 km/h), flying at an altitude of 110,000 feet (33,528 meters). The X-43A is an unmanned experimental aircraft, designed to send payloads into space.

HEAT SHIELDS

The nose, tail, and wings of the X-43A are covered with a heat-resistant, carbon-based material. This protects it from the high temperatures caused by friction as it travels through the air.

AERODYNAMICS

The body of the X-43A is shaped to create its own lift, rather than relying on the lift provided by wings. It is surprisingly stable.

FUEL

The engine runs on hydrogen fuel. This is ignited with air forced at high speed into the scramjet's air intake.

SILANE TANK

Pyrophoric silane, which ignites on contact with air, is used to start the engine.

Flight management unit

Battery

SENSOR UNIT

This detects any changes to the airflow entering the engine's air intake and instructs the linked control system to make the necessary adjustments to compensate. Reliable air flow is vital for scramjet engines.

Scramjet

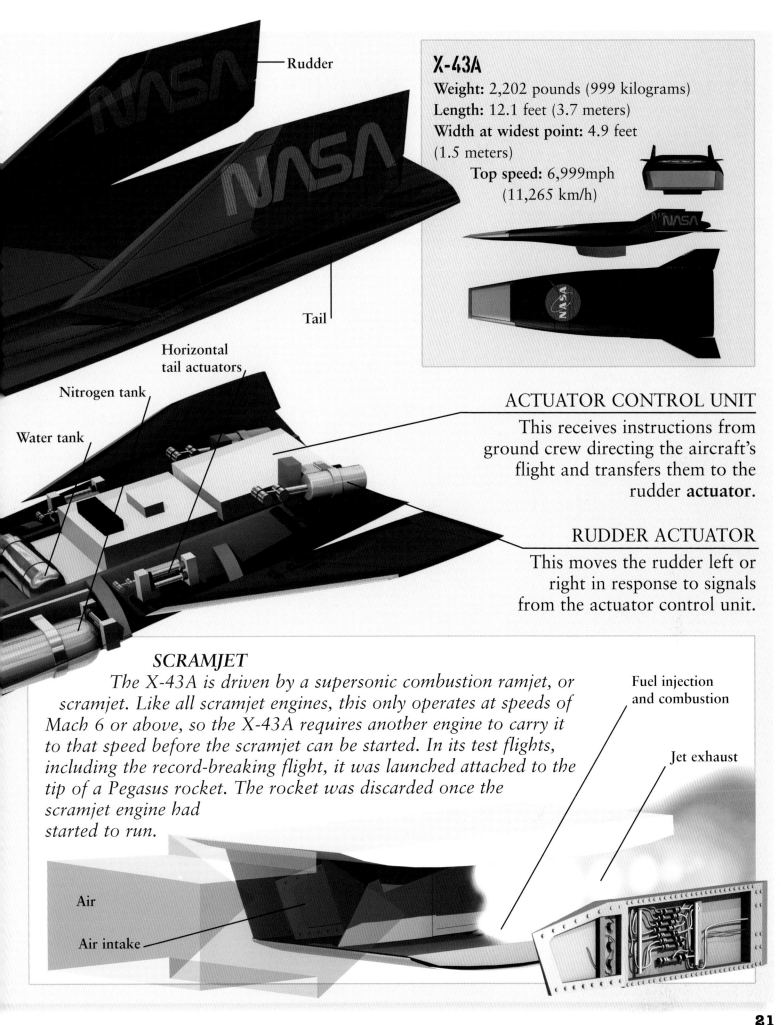

Rudder

Tail

Horizontal tail actuators

Nitrogen tank

Water tank

X-43A

Weight: 2,202 pounds (999 kilograms)
Length: 12.1 feet (3.7 meters)
Width at widest point: 4.9 feet (1.5 meters)
Top speed: 6,999mph (11,265 km/h)

ACTUATOR CONTROL UNIT

This receives instructions from ground crew directing the aircraft's flight and transfers them to the rudder **actuator**.

RUDDER ACTUATOR

This moves the rudder left or right in response to signals from the actuator control unit.

SCRAMJET

The X-43A is driven by a supersonic combustion ramjet, or scramjet. Like all scramjet engines, this only operates at speeds of Mach 6 or above, so the X-43A requires another engine to carry it to that speed before the scramjet can be started. In its test flights, including the record-breaking flight, it was launched attached to the tip of a Pegasus rocket. The rocket was discarded once the scramjet engine had started to run.

Fuel injection and combustion

Jet exhaust

Air

Air intake

VIRGIN ATLANTIC GLOBALFLYER

The Virgin Atlantic GlobalFlyer holds the record for the fastest nonstop flight around the world without refueling. Starting on February 28 and finishing on March 3, 2005, the pilot, Steve Fossett, made the journey in sixty-seven hours, with an average speed of 367 mph (590.7 km/h) per minute. The GlobalFlyer was designed by the aerospace engineer Burt Rutan, who had also designed the previous record holder, Voyager.

VIRGIN ATLANTIC GLOBALFLYER
Wingspan: 114 feet (34.75 meters)
Length: 44 feet (13.44 meters)
Height: 13 feet (4 meters)
Top speed: 195.7 mph (315 km/h)
Weight (empty): 3,699 pounds (1,678 kilograms)
Weight (full): 22,099 pounds (10,024 kilograms)

WINGS

The wings are built from carbon fiber, making them lightweight but strong. When fully loaded with fuel the wings flexed up to 7.8 feet (2.4 meters).

COCKPIT

The cruising height of 44,947 feet (13,700 meters) means that the 6.8 foot (2.1 meter) long cabin has to be pressurized.

FUEL TANKS

There are thirteen fuel tanks—one in the main fuselage, two in each boom, and four in each wing. Between them they can hold 18,016 pounds (8,172 kilograms) of jet fuel. Before taking the nonstop round-the-world speed record, this plane made the longest ever flight without refueling—25,766 miles (41,467 kilometers).

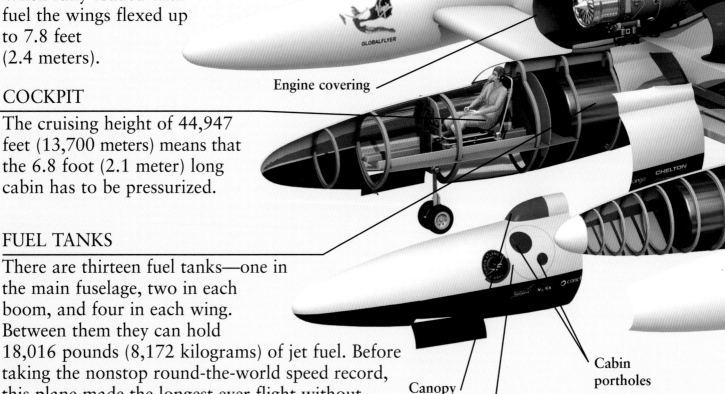

Engine covering

Canopy

Door

Cabin portholes

ENGINE

The GlobalFlyer is powered by a single Williams International FJ44-3 ATW turbofan engine, chosen for its small size and fuel efficiency. It normally uses standard jet fuel, which needs heaters to keep it from freezing at high altitudes. To save the weight of heaters, Rutan adjusted the engine to burn JP-3 fuel instead, which has a lower freezing point.

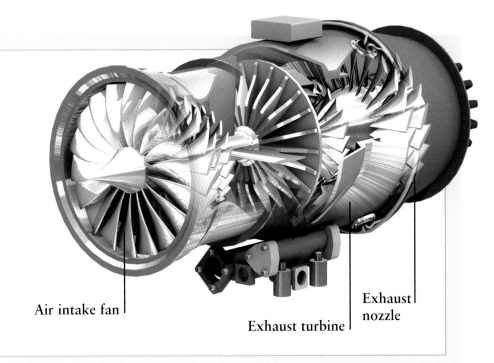

Air intake fan

Exhaust turbine

Exhaust nozzle

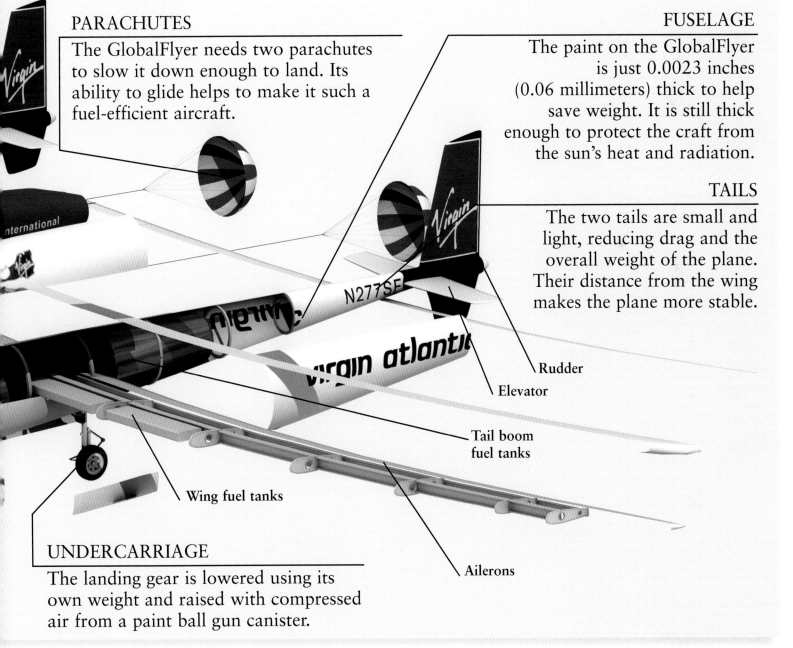

PARACHUTES

The GlobalFlyer needs two parachutes to slow it down enough to land. Its ability to glide helps to make it such a fuel-efficient aircraft.

FUSELAGE

The paint on the GlobalFlyer is just 0.0023 inches (0.06 millimeters) thick to help save weight. It is still thick enough to protect the craft from the sun's heat and radiation.

TAILS

The two tails are small and light, reducing drag and the overall weight of the plane. Their distance from the wing makes the plane more stable.

Rudder

Elevator

Tail boom fuel tanks

Wing fuel tanks

Ailerons

UNDERCARRIAGE

The landing gear is lowered using its own weight and raised with compressed air from a paint ball gun canister.

AIRBUS A380

The Airbus A380 is the world's largest passenger airliner. It made its maiden flight on April 27, 2005, and its first commercial flight on October 25, 2007. Airbus is a European corporation that makes different parts of the plane in different countries. For example, the wings are built in the United Kingdom and the tail is built in Spain.

PASSENGER DECKS
The A380 has two passenger decks, with sections for first class, business class, and economy class passengers. The number of passengers varies from just over five hundred with three classes to more than 850 with only economy class.

Internal structure

Stairway

FLIGHT DECK
As on other Airbus planes, the A380 uses a "fly-by-wire" (computer-operated) system.

Radar

AVIONICS
The A380 uses Integrated Modular Avionics, previously used in advanced military aircraft. It has a powerful network systems server that holds all the information and displays it via Liquid Crystal Display (LCD) panels.

Baggage containers

BAGGAGE HOLD
Beneath the passenger decks is the baggage compartment, where luggage is stored. In the future, shops, restaurants, and other recreational facilities may be housed in this area.

UNDERCARRIAGE
The main undercarriage has twenty wheels, each 4.59 feet (1.4 meters) in diameter. Two wheels under the aircraft's nose steer the plane.

Outer skin

AIRBUS A380

Wingspan: 261.8 feet (79.8 meters)
Length: 239.5 feet (73 meters)
Height: 79 feet (24.1 meters)
Top speed: 633 mph (1,020 km/h)
Maximum payload: 100 tons
(90.8 metric tons)

Elevator

Fuel tank

Tail

WINGLET

At the end of each wing is a winglet. In flight, air passing over the wings becomes turbulent and swirls off the wing's tip. The winglets dissipate this, reduce drag, and make the plane more fuel efficient.

Engine

ENGINE

*The Airbus 380 has four **turbofan jet engines**—two mounted on the underside of each wing. Most are Rolls-Royce Trent 900 engines. Some have the Engine Alliance GP7000. Both types of engine weigh more than 6 tons.*

Jet exhaust nozzle

Compressor

Intake fan turbine blades

Intake fan shroud

Airflow guidance cone

WINGS

Each enormous wing measures 118 feet (36 meters). As well as housing the plane's landing gear, they hold fuel—a total of 49,237 gallons (186,386 liters).

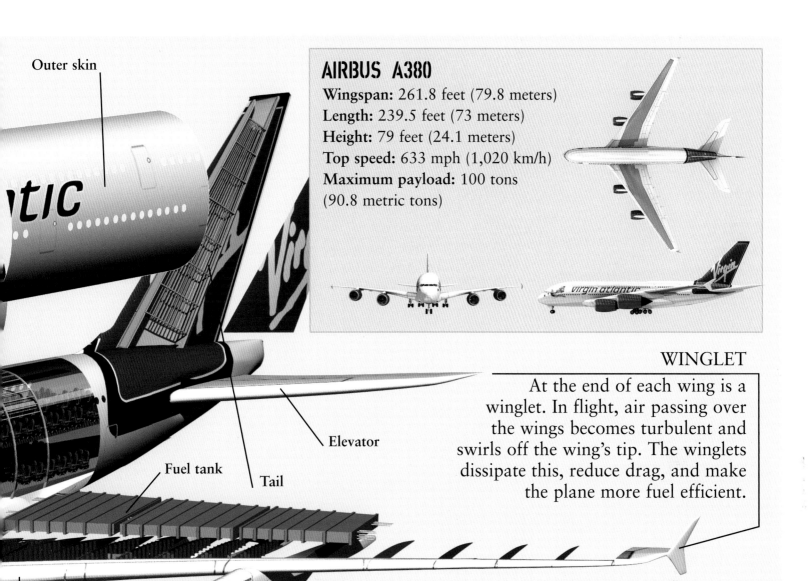

BUGATTI VEYRON

When it was introduced in 2005, the Bugatti Veyron was the world's fastest production road car, capable of reaching 252 mph (407 km/h). It accelerates from 0 to 60 mph (0 to 99 km/h) in 2.5 seconds, and takes 24 seconds to reach 200 mph (322 km/h) from a standing start. A total of three hundred are to be built, each costing approximately $1,635,840.

BUGATTI VEYRON

Length: 14.7 feet (4.5 meters)
Width: 6.5 feet (2 meters)
Height: 3.9 feet (1.2 meters)
Weight: 2.07 tons (1.88 metric tons)
Top speed: 252.8 mph (407 km/h)

TAIL WING

When the car reaches 136 mph (220 km/h) the tail wing automatically lifts into place. Like an upside-down aircraft wing it pushes the rear of the car onto the road, giving the wheels more grip. When the driver brakes, the wing changes its angle and becomes an air brake.

SUSPENSION

At top speed, hydraulic motors lower the car's suspension, so it is just 3.5 inches (8.9 centimeters) above the road.

Gearbox

Fuel tank

BRAKES

The Veyron's brake disks are made from a compound of silicon and carbon—the same material covers the Space Shuttle's nose and is used in bulletproof vests. The brakes bring the Veyron from 252.8 mph (400 km/h) to a halt in less than 10 seconds.

WHEELS

The rear tires are 14.4 inches (36.6 centimeters) wide and the front tires 9.4 inches (24.1 centimeters). When completely flat they can still run for 124 miles (201 kilometers) at 49 mph (80 km/h).

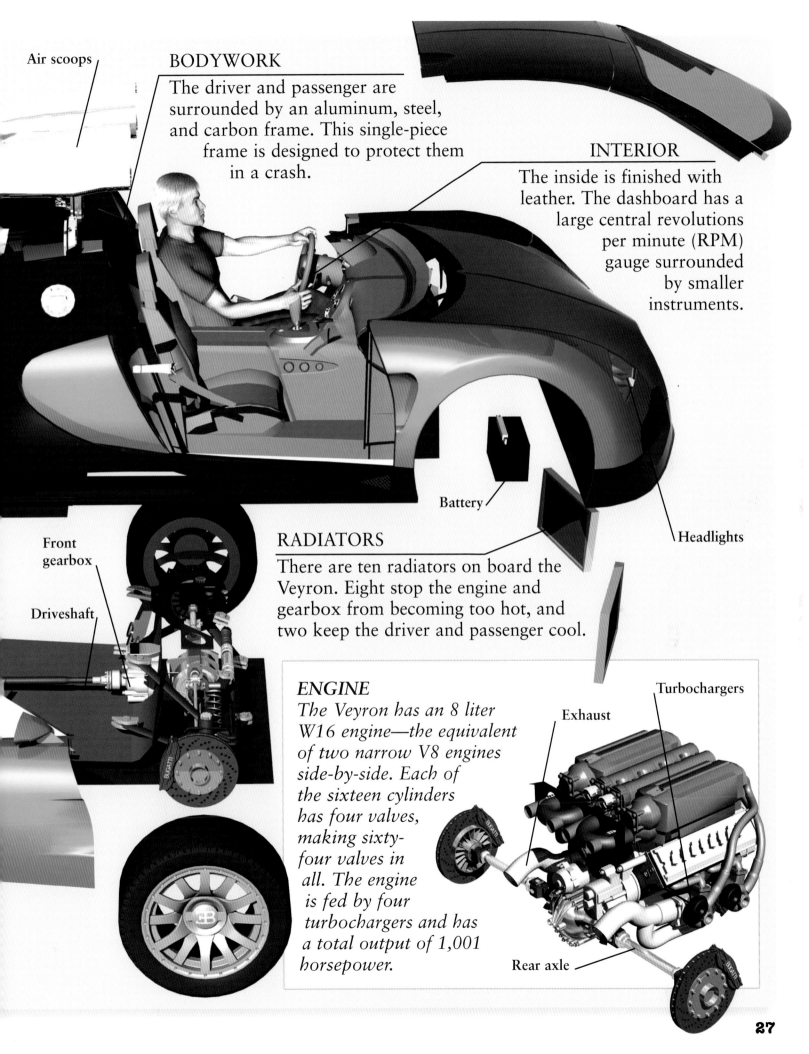

Air scoops

BODYWORK

The driver and passenger are surrounded by an aluminum, steel, and carbon frame. This single-piece frame is designed to protect them in a crash.

INTERIOR

The inside is finished with leather. The dashboard has a large central revolutions per minute (RPM) gauge surrounded by smaller instruments.

Battery

RADIATORS

There are ten radiators on board the Veyron. Eight stop the engine and gearbox from becoming too hot, and two keep the driver and passenger cool.

Front gearbox

Driveshaft

Headlights

ENGINE

The Veyron has an 8 liter W16 engine—the equivalent of two narrow V8 engines side-by-side. Each of the sixteen cylinders has four valves, making sixty-four valves in all. The engine is fed by four turbochargers and has a total output of 1,001 horsepower.

Turbochargers

Exhaust

Rear axle

TGV 4402

TGV 4402 is the fastest train ever to run on conventional rails. On April 3, 2007, it set a new world record speed of 357 mph (574.8 km/h). TGV 4402 is a one-of-a-kind train that was specially modified to make the world record attempt. It is based on the TGV POS, which routinely carries passengers through France at up to 198.8 mph (320 km/h).

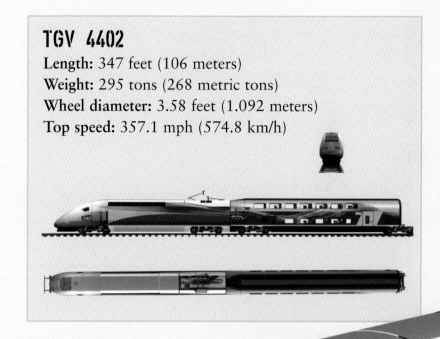

TGV 4402
Length: 347 feet (106 meters)
Weight: 295 tons (268 metric tons)
Wheel diameter: 3.58 feet (1.092 meters)
Top speed: 357.1 mph (574.8 km/h)

Cooling tanks

DRIVER'S CAB
The cab of TGV 4402 has a comfortable, soft seat for the driver, surrounded by controls.

TRANSFORMERS
These convert the electrical power gathered by the pantograph to a voltage the train's engines can use.

POWER PACK
This receives electricity from the transformers and uses it to drive the wheels of the locomotive.

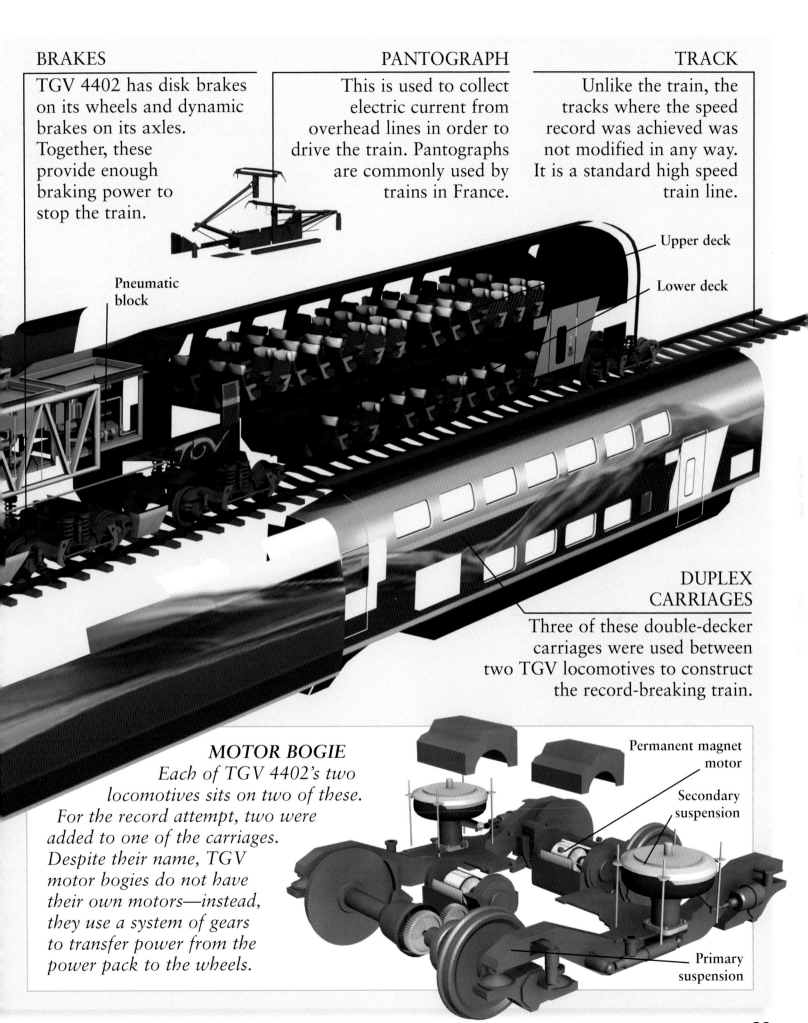

BRAKES

TGV 4402 has disk brakes on its wheels and dynamic brakes on its axles. Together, these provide enough braking power to stop the train.

PANTOGRAPH

This is used to collect electric current from overhead lines in order to drive the train. Pantographs are commonly used by trains in France.

TRACK

Unlike the train, the tracks where the speed record was achieved was not modified in any way. It is a standard high speed train line.

Pneumatic block

Upper deck

Lower deck

DUPLEX CARRIAGES

Three of these double-decker carriages were used between two TGV locomotives to construct the record-breaking train.

MOTOR BOGIE

Each of TGV 4402's two locomotives sits on two of these. For the record attempt, two were added to one of the carriages. Despite their name, TGV motor bogies do not have their own motors—instead, they use a system of gears to transfer power from the power pack to the wheels.

Permanent magnet motor

Secondary suspension

Primary suspension

MORE RECORD BREAKERS

Records are constantly broken as advances in technology are made. Electronics and nanotechnology (the study of the control of matter on an atomic and molecular scale) are getting tinier and materials for construction are getting lighter and stronger.

The smallest gas engine can sit on a fingertip and run for two years on a small squirt of lighter fuel. The smallest motor ever built was a gold rotor on a nanotube shaft that could ride on the back of a virus. At the other end of the scale, engines are built to enormous sizes. The most powerful diesel engine in the world is the Wartsila-Sulzer RTA96-C, designed for large container ships. It stands five stories high, at 44.2 feet (13.5 meters), is 89.5 feet (27.3 meters) long, and weighs over 2,535 tons (2,300 metric tons).

CONCORDE
In 1992, a Concorde made the fastest nonorbital circumnavigation, taking 32 hours, 49 minutes, and 3 seconds to fly around the world.

APOLLO 10
Its crew traveled at 24,790 mph (39,897 km/h).

FREEDOM OF THE SEAS
This is the world's largest cruise ship. It can carry 3,634 passengers.

BAGGER 288
This is the world's largest tracked vehicle. Unlike NASA's Crawler-Transporter, it is powered by an external source.

GLOSSARY

actuator
A mechanical device that controls the movement of a mechanism or system.

alloy
A mixture of two or more metals, or a metal and another chemical element, such as carbon.

avionics
An abbreviation of "aviation electronics." The electrical and electronic systems that enable an aircraft or similar vehicle to fly.

carbon fiber
A lightweight but strong material made from microscopic carbon threads.

chassis
The frame that forms the basic skeleton of a motor vehicle. The axles and bodywork are attached to the chassis.

coupling rods
Rods that connect the driving wheels of a locomotive.

diesel
A type of fuel used by motor vehicles. Diesel is normally oil-based but may also be derived from organic matter.

electric traction motor
An electric motor that drives the wheels of a machine.

fuselage
The central body of an aircraft, to which the wings and tail are attached.

gauge
A measurement, often the thickness of a material, diameter of a slender object, or the distance between the rails of a railroad.

hydraulic
Operated by a liquid under high pressure, such as water or oil.

infrared
Electromagnetic radiation just beyond the red end of the light spectrum. Infrared radiation is given off by objects warmer than the surrounding air.

locomotive
A self-propelled engine that pushes or pulls a train along tracks. A locomotive may be powered by steam, diesel, or electricity.

National Aeronautics and Space Administration (NASA)
The U.S. government agency responsible for the nation's space program.

payload
Cargo, such as equipment and satellites, that is carried by the vehicle.

rudder
A moveable flap used for steering an airplane or boat.

sound barrier
An imaginary line that is crossed when traveling at speeds greater than the speed of sound, which is 767 mph (1,235 km/h).

supersonic
Faster than the speed of sound, which is 767 mph (1,235 km/h).

tender
A wagon designed to carry coal and water for a steam locomotive.

turbofan jet engine
A jet engine with a fan that blows air onto the burner to provide extra thrust.

undercarriage
The wheels and landing gear of an aircraft.

INDEX